T0011946

THE LITTLE GUIDE TO

# MADONNA

This edition published in 2023 by OH!
An Imprint of Welbeck Non-Fiction Limited,
part of Welbeck Publishing Group.
Offices in: London – 20 Mortimer Street, London W1T 3JW
and Sydney – Level 17, 207 Kent St, Sydney NSW 2000 Australia
www.welbeckpublishing.com

Compilation text © Welbeck Non-Fiction Limited 2023
Design © Welbeck Non-Fiction Limited 2023

ISBN 978-1-80069-527-6

Compiled and written by: Malcolm Croft
Editorial: Victoria Denne
Project manager: Russell Porter
Design: Tony Seddon
Production: Jess Brisley

A CIP catalogue record for this book is available from the British Library

Printed in China

10 9 8 7 6 5 4 3 2 1

# THE LITTLE GUIDE TO
# MADONNA

## EXPRESS YOURSELF

# CONTENTS

# INTRODUCTION

Pop music's most enduring monoym, Madonna requires absolutely no introduction from anyone and hasn't done since she burst out onto the world's stage in 1983 with the release of her debut album, *Madonna*, a dance-pop classic action-packed with timeless, melody-laden bangers. Within ten years of its release, Madonna became an object of obsession, a pin-up…and the most influential, and bestselling, female musical artist of all time.

Ever since that daring debut, this pioneering and provocative popstar has tickled, teased and titillated the tied-up inhibitions of music, film, art, fashion and culture to the point of wild climax, redefined the zeitgeist multiple times and, without a doubt, kickstarted a female revolution in pop music, echoes of which we see everywhere today. Famed and feared in equal measure, Madonna has meant many things to many people: gay icon, Hollywood actress, activist, entrepreneur, children's book author, DJ, film director/producer and, most importantly now, a mother to six children. All while selling hundreds of millions of albums and singles.

This Little Book of wit and wisdom has everything a Madonna fan deserves, a tiny tome crammed with killer quotes and wisecrackin' zingers that celebrate the singer's greatest adventures, accomplishments and "scandals", as well as her life in music, all told through her own authentic practicising of what she preaches.

So, Madonna, Queen of Pop, what are you waiting for? Don't just stand there, let's get to it, strike a pose, there's nothing to it...it's time to open your heart, get into the groove and take a bow, your fans are waiting for you to express yourself...

# CHAPTER
## ONE

# WHO'S
# THAT GIRL?

Today, Madonna still revels in the
provocation and power she holds as much
as she did when she was a supernova.
And she remains as relevant as the mother
of reinvention as ever. By consistently
breaking the mould at every turn, this
multi-talented, entrepreneurial singer-
songwriter lit the path for every popstar
who followed her.

Her 1987 movie, and soundtrack, asked
her fans to answer the question: *Who's
that girl?* But have we ever really spent any
time in bed with the *real* Madonna? In her
own words, let's go find out…

I am not reinventing myself; I am going through layers and revealing myself. I am on a journey, an adventure that's constantly changing shape.

Madonna, on her reputation for reinvention, promoting *Ray of Light*, interview with *USA Today*, 1998.

"
I want to be like Gandhi,
and Martin Luther King,
and John Lennon... but
I want to stay alive.
"

Madonna, on being an icon, interview with
Sirius Radio, February 16, 2007.

66

Life is a paradox and you have
to embrace that in your work
and your belief systems... You
can't be a literalist, and that's
the trouble that people always
find themselves in. That's
why people always hit a wall
with any of my stuff, because
you can't take it literally.

99

Madonna, on literally being taken literally, interview
with *Dazed & Confused*, April 2008.

It has taken me a long time to realize money doesn't bring happiness. I spent 15 years of my life thinking about myself, thinking about everything from the point of view of: 'What is in it for me?'

Madonna, on fame and fortune, interview with *Grazia* magazine, June 27, 2005.

When my daughter was
born, I was born again.

Madonna, on motherhood, interview with
*New York Times*, June 2019.

66

How many years have
I been doing this? 36?
Zero fucks given.

99

Madonna, on why she's endured so long, interview
with *iHeartRadio ICONS*, June 2019.

I am a brunette and
sometimes I just like to
match my pubic hair
sometimes. People who
have nothing better to do
than talk about my hair
colour have no lives.

Madonna, on the media overanalyzing her
appearance after dying her hair black, interview
with *Interview*, April 2003.

I'm not going to change the world in a day. I don't know, maybe it never will be where men and women will be equal. It just seems like as long as women are the ones that give birth to children, it'll never really change.

Madonna, on gender equality, interview with *Rolling Stone*, September 1987.

For years, I never had any money, and I never had any help, and having to struggle to survive has made me as tough as I am and turned me into the bitch that most people think I am! But it was meant to be, because here I am.

Madonna, on her early struggles defining her strength, interview with *Time Out*, January 1989.

What fuels my ambition
is the desire to be
heard. And to find my
mother, I suppose.

"

Madonna, on her ambitions and her mother,
interview with *Vanity Fair*, December 1986.

"

I do think of myself as a queen, but I don't think I'm the only queen. There's room for other queens. We reign over different kingdoms.

"

Madonna, on being called the "Queen of Pop", interview with *Rolling Stone* magazine, March 2015.

I don't value diamonds. I rarely wear jewellery. I'm perfectly happy to muck around in a pair of pants and wellies. Sometimes my daughter gets angry because I go to school with her, wearing my tracksuit, and she says, 'Please can't you just wear normal clothes?' I think she wants me to be a Yummy Mummy but that's not me.

Madonna, on not being a material girl, interview with *Grazia* magazine, June 27, 2005.

I always felt too guilty to ask my father for any money. I had turned down a scholarship at the University of Michigan to come to New York so I couldn't expect much sympathy for starving there when I could be living wonderfully in Michigan and going to an Ivy League school and blah blah blah.

Madonna, on her family's wealth, interview with *Rock Video*, February 1985.

"

I played with my Barbie dolls all the time. I definitely lived out my fantasies with them. I dressed them up in sarongs and mini-skirts and stuff. They were having sex all the time. I rubbed her and Ken together a lot.

"

Madonna, on her favourite childhood toy, interview with *Record Magazine*, March 1985.

If anybody wants to know,
I never fucked anyone to
get anywhere. Never.

Madonna, on her success, interview with
*Record Magazine*, March 1985.

I meant to poke a hole in the whole idea of sexuality. What I predicted would happen, happened: everyone went out and bought the book, it sold out, then everyone slagged it off, which to me is an absolute reflection of public attitudes towards sex in America. It did what I intended to do.

Madonna, on her *Sex* book, interview with *Juice*, April 1998.

We're all prostitutes
in our own way.

Madonna, on selling ourselves, interview with
*Interview* magazine, June 1993.

66

This is what a 56-year-old ass looks like, motherfuckers.

99

Madonna, on baring all for a *Rolling Stone* photoshoot in 2015, interview with *Rolling Stone* magazine, March 2015.

They thought they would wake up one day and I'd go away. But I'm not going to go away. They keep waking up and I keep not going away. And that just pisses them off. In the beginning they thought that I was the flavour of the month. A one-act Disco Dolly who was just going to pop in and pop out. It took them forever to accept the fact that I could write music and that I have something to contribute in the world of music.

Madonna, on forever being misunderstood by the media, interview with *Time Out*, January 1989.

I'm not going to say that
I've never slept with a
woman, but I love men.

99

Madonna, on sexuality and love, interview with
*Los Angeles Times*, October 23, 1994.

Everyone's down on the
'80s right now, but I thought
the '80s was fabulous
and I'm sure Boy George
would agree with me.

Madonna, on the 1980s, interview with
*Q Magazine*, March 1998.

**"**

# My pussy is the temple of learning.

**"**

Madonna, on places of worship, interview with
*New York Times*, June 2019

"

The whole point of being in a relationship and having children is that you learn to love… unconditionally. That's the best contribution to making the world a better place. It's so nice sometimes just to go into my children's bedrooms and listen to them breathe. It has forced me to get out of myself.

"

Madonna, on being a mother, interview with *Grazia* magazine, June 27, 2005.

It's psedo-Puerto Rican punk rock freak out. A Motorcycle baby. It's a combination of my two oldest fantasies. One was to be Nancy Sinatra; the other was to be a nun.

Madonna, on her stage style, interview with *Island* magazine, October 1983.

# CHAPTER
# TWO

# EN VOGUE

Madonna blew the bloody doors to the 1990s clean off with the release of her era-defining track, "Vogue", a killer dance epic-cum-mission statement that defined her as the biggest artist, and celebrity, in the world.

At the height of her superstardom, and her quest to find her place in this world, Madonna spoke about her fame, fortune, family, fans and fears as well as her cheeky desire to prod and poke the status quo into submission. Read all about it…

##### 66

I look and I say, 'Wow, what a very young, innocent, naive little girl,' but I also see that I was having a good time, and I'm proud of myself.

##### 99

Madonna, on her early fame and photoshoots, interview with *Juice*, April 1998.

Hunger for knowledge.
A desire to be adventurous,
to learn things, to grow.
Curiosity.

Madonna, on her best features, interview with
*Juice*, April 1998.

Madonna's best-selling album is her greatest hits compilation, the brilliantly titled *The Immaculate Collection*. To date, it has sold more than 30 million copies.

Next in line is her third album, *True Blue*, which remains her most successful studio album, shifting 24 million copies.

66

I came from a small town in
the middle of nowhere without
any particular education
and no special training in
anything. It wasn't really
about ambition: I just wanted
to go out into the world. I
wanted a little adventure.

99

Madonna, on her call to adventure, interview with
*Juice*, April 1998.

Believe it or not, I'm at my most creative when I'm standing at a microphone and the pressure's on.

Madonna, on her lyrical creativity, interview with *The Face*, August 2000.

"

Writing is a very intimate thing, especially when you write lyrics and sing them in front of someone for the first time. It's like a really embarrassing situation. To me, singing is almost like crying, and you have to really know someone before you can start crying in front of them.

"

Madonna, on writing lyrics, interview with
*Observer Music Monthly*, November 2005.

I used to go to this club in New York, Danceteria, and I kept bringing my demos to the DJ. So all music for me begins with the DJ taking my first record, 'Everybody', and thinking it's good enough to play to everyone to dance to.

Madonna, on her first song "Everybody", interview with *Observer Music Monthly*, November 2005.

# When I stop thinking about myself all the time and put other people before me on a regular basis, that's real freedom.

Madonna, on freedom, interview with *Interview* magazine, April 2008.

66

One day my art teacher came over to me and hit me over the head with this rolled-up piece of paper and told me, 'You're terrible! You're never going to be an artist. You're a showgirl, get out of here.'

99

Madonna, on her earliest of critics, interview with *Rolling Stone* magazine, March 2015.

**"**

My first pop idol was
Nancy Sinatra. Go-go
boots, miniskirt, blond hair,
fake eyelashes – she was
cool. My first movie idol
was Marilyn Monroe. Jesus
Christ was like a movie star,
my favorite idol of all.

**"**

Madonna, on her earliest idols, interview with
*Spin*, May 1985.

**"**

I go running everyday in my neighbourhood. People bother me all the time, but it's important for me to stay in touch with – it sounds clichéd – with the street. I didn't struggle my way out of Michigan so I could crawl into a hole.

**"**

Madonna, on staying in touch with the street, interview with *Songtalk*, June 1989.

God seems to be there whenever things are really horrible. I do try to remind myself – I know this sounds corny – to be thankful for things when they're good, to be conscious of God.

Madonna, on God and religion, interview with *Rolling Stone*, June 1991.

# 13

The total number of
UK No.1s Madonna has
had, the most a
female artist has ever
achieved.

My stepmother told me about sex, and I remember I was horrified. I was 10 and had just started my period. I remember my stepmother was in the kitchen, and I was washing dishes. Every time she said the word penis, I'd turn the water on really hard so it would drown out what she said. I thought what she was telling me was absolutely horrifying. And I hated the word. I just hated the whole thing.

Madonna, on being first told about sex, interview with *Rolling Stone*, June 1991.

When you're not popular
and everyone seems to
have turned on you, you
kind of have a freedom
to do whatever you want,
whenever you want,
because you don't have
to please everyone.

Madonna, on being unpopular, interview with
*Q Magazine*, March 1998.

66

If I'm in a car or I go into
a restaurant, I'm out
somewhere, and one of
my songs starts playing, I
just go, 'Ugh!' – because
I've had to hear it five
billion times already, and
I want to escape that.

99

Madonna, on listening to her early material, interview
with *New York Times*, June 2019

"

I used to draw people naked all the time in my art class and my nun teachers used to tell me I had to put clothes on them. So I just drew lines around their bodies. See-through clothes.

"

Madonna, on her Catholic upbringing, interview with *Island* magazine, October 1983.

I never saw naked bodies.
I never saw my parents
naked. When I was seventeen
I hadn't even seen a penis.

Madonna, on her conservative childhood, interview
with *Island* magazine, October 1983.

People didn't get it. But if you're waiting for me to say I regret doing it, you'll be waiting a very long time.

Madonna, on the now-infamous *Sex* book, interview with *Cosmopolitan*, February 1996.

**"**

I've been in four very successful films – *Desperately Seeking Susan*, *Dick Tracy*, *A League of Their Own*, and *Truth or Dare*. I've also been in four or five stinkers – some of which weren't my films at all, though they were promoted as such.

**"**

Madonna, on her acting career, interview with *Cosmopolitan*, February 1996.

Most of the time I definitely don't act older than a teenager. And that's a good thing.

Madonna, on feeling forever young, interview with *Q Magazine*, May 2008.

"

I was attracted to creative people. I don't want to be the smartest person in the room, I want to be the dumbest in the room. I want to be surrounded by other thinking people who are going to say something that makes me think, 'Oh, my god that's an amazing idea. Why didn't I think of that?'

"

Madonna, on surrounding herself with smart people, interview with *Interview* magazine, January 2015.

**"**

I was surprised with how people reacted to 'Like a Virgin'. Everyone else interpreted it as 'I don't want to be a virgin anymore, fuck my brains out!' That's not what I sang at all.

**"**

Madonna, on "Like a Virgin", interview with *Rolling Stone*, September 1987.

When Madonna famously arrived in New York in 1978 with only $35 in her pocket, she got a job selling dough at Dunkin' Donuts.

However, she was fired in her first week for reportedly using the jelly squirting machine for squirting, well, not donuts.

People have this idea that if you're sexual and beautiful and provocative, then there's nothing else you could possibly offer. People have always had that image about women. And while it might have seemed like I was behaving in a stereotypical way, at the same time, I was also masterminding it. I was in control of everything I was doing, and I think that when people realized that, it confused them.

Madonna, on being the mastermind of her own creation, interview with *Rolling Stone*, September 1987.

Being a rebel or being a pioneer, it's not terribly much fun, I have to say, because you become a target for everyone's fears. You have to be incredibly resilient and there were times when I wished that I hadn't been so outspoken, because it was so exhausting to constantly have to defend myself.

Madonna, on being a pioneer, interview with *Q Magazine*, March 1998.

I woke up one day and realized that smart, sassy girls who accomplish a lot and have their own cash are independent... and really frightening to men.

Madonna, on independent women, interview with *Interview* magazine, March 2001.

66

When I first moved to New York I wanted to be a dancer, I danced professionally for years, living a hand-to-mouth existence. I never tapped into nightlife, all I knew was dancers, we went to bed early and got up early. Then I met this guy, as one does, and he brought me to a nightclub [called Pete's Place] and I was like, 'Wow'. I didn't know you could just walk into a club and start dancing by yourself. I thought someone had to ask you.

99

Madonna, on her first dancefloor/nightclub experience, interview with *Observer Music Monthly*, November 2005.

---

**"**

# Yes, I am the first Spice Girl.

**"**

Madonna, on girl power, interview with
*Juice*, April 1998.

---

Obviously, I haven't hit my stride in movies, but let me say this: I'm not particularly interested in becoming a great big movie star. I am interested in becoming a good actress. If one comes with the other, that's fine. But I don't spend my life mourning my flops.

Madonna, on her flops, interview with *Cosmopolitan*, February 1996.

Madonna performed at the very first MTV Video Music Awards with her unforgettable (read: scandalous) performance of "Like a Virgin" in 1984.

She wore a white bridesmaid dress (read: corset) draped in crucifixes. The performance, without a doubt, inspired millions of future artists to be just like her.

66

I remember from when I was very, very young, being really attracted to men, and being real flirtatious. The power of my femininity and charm, I remember it was just something I had, that I'd been given, you know what I mean? From the age of five I remember being able to affect people that way.

99

Madonna, on her flirtatious manner, interview with *Record Magazine*, March 1985.

---

**"**

# Fantasies are essential. Without fantasies I would have died of starvation.

**"**

Madonna, on fantasies, interview with
*Island* magazine, October 1983.

---

66

Everyone slagged it off without having seen it. Don't you think that's absurd? That's how the media is: eventually they have to pull you down.

99

Madonna, on the critical and commercial failure of her movie *Swept Away*, interview with *Q Magazine*, April 2003.

Let's talk about economics:
I know there's a lot of
competition in the world of
magazines and newspapers and
they have to make headlines
be sensational and sell, and
saying bad things about me is
going to sell more papers than
writing good things about me.

Madonna, on the tabloid media, interview with
*Observer Music Monthly*, November 2005.

66

Since the very beginning of my career I've always promoted freedom of expression and embracing the idea of being different. Independence of thought; fighting any kind of oppression. And also: I'm a diva. I think 'queer nation' and 'diva' just go together. The diva in them recognized the diva in me. All my banging dancefloor tunes? Well, yes. That goes without saying.

99

Madonna, on being a gay icon, interview with *Q Magazine*, May 2008.

# CHAPTER
# THREE

# AGENT PROVOCATEUR

Over a stunning 40-year career,
Madonna has never held herself back
from preaching to papa what she practises
(which is a lot), leaving a lovely legacy
of witty one-liners and controversy-baiting
quotes to keep her legions of adoring
fans unlikely to be ever lost for her words.
As she once said, "Fame is a
great aphrodisiac."

So too, it seemed, was provocation…

Why can I not be sexual and be intelligent? Why can't I strut around onstage like Mick Jagger and not be pigeonholed as a bimbo? Why?

Madonna, on the double standards of sexism, interview with *Rolling Stone* magazine, March 2015.

My first album was a total aerobics records. I make records with aerobics in mind. When I'm mad or have a fight with my boyfriend, I work out.

Madonna, on the importance of exercise, interview with *Spin*, May 1985.

I thought it was sick. I thought it was sick and perverted and that's why I liked it. Sick and perverted always appeals to me.

Madonna, on hearing "Like a Prayer" for the first time, interview with *Songtalk*, June 1989.

It's not really that I thrive on controversy. It's that I think it's necessary. I think art should be controversial. I think it should make people think. I mean, everything is just kind of opium for the masses. It puts people in a trance. I think it's good to hit people over the head with this stuff and make them question their own beliefs.

Madonna, on art as controversy, interview with *Songtalk*, June 1989.

Madonna has released 15 studio albums, selling a total of more than 300 million records, a feat no doubt never to be matched by any other female artist.

**"**

My memories of my mother drift in and out. When I turned thirty, which was the age my mother was when she died, I just flipped because I kept thinking I'm now outliving my mother. I thought something horrible was going to happen to me. Like this is it, my time is up.

**"**

Madonna, on outliving her mother, interview with *Vanity Fair*, April 1990.

You cannot be an
inspiration to people or
a role model unless you
have a point of view.

Madonna, on being an inspiring role model, interview
with *Q Magazine*, December 1994.

66
# Power is a great aphrodisiac.
99

Madonna, on power, interview with *Q Magazine*,
March 1998.

> **"**
>
> When I was living on the Lower East Side… I didn't see many concerts. I knew about Debbie Harry and Chrissie Hynde and the Talking Heads and David Bowie, but there was no pressure for me to sound a certain way, to look a certain way. That's important, because it allowed me to develop as an artist and to be pure, without any influences. What I try to do now is to remember that girl.
>
> **"**

Madonna, on her lack of influences and early career, interview with *New York Times*, June 2019.

66

I grew up in an all-black neighborhood and I wanted to be a black girl. There was something about me that was so much freer than the white kids I knew and they didn't go to the Catholic schools I went to.

99

Madonna, on her childhood in Bay City, Michigan, interview with *Island* magazine, October 1983.

Madonna has appeared in nearly 20 films since her acting debut in *Desperately Seeking Susan* in 1985.

Her lead role in the 1996 film adaptation of the musical *Evita* was heaped with accolade and praise. For her performance, she won the Golden Globe for Best Actress in a Musical or Comedy. Can you name the other movies?

66

Men who are with me have to endure my image as well as the reality of people taking that image literally and throwing themselves at me. So I'm always reassuring my men. I say, 'You're the one. I'm here with you.'

99

Madonna, on jealousy, interview with *Cosmopolitan*, February 1996.

Quite frankly, before I met Guy [Ritchie], I really had my head up my arse as far as relationships go. I wasn't a very giving person. Having children, really falling in love, head and shoulders, it changes you. There's no time for nonsense anymore.

Madonna, on how love and motherhood has changed her, interview with *Q Magazine*, April 2003.

Fame is a by-product. Fame is something that happens because you do work that speaks to people and people want to know about your work. But I don't think one should ever aspire to being famous.

Madonna, on fame, interview with *Q Magazine*, May 2008.

**66**

You forgive people a lot when you're distracted by how gorgeous they are.

**99**

Madonna, on good-looking people, interview with *Interview* magazine, March 2001.

There's no law that says that you cannot be a spiritual person and a sexual person. In fact, if you have the right consciousness, sex is like a prayer. It can be a divine experience. So why do they have to be disassociated with one another?

Madonna, on sex and religion as bedfellows, interview with *Rolling Stone* magazine, March 2015.

I'm just a scruffy, tough girl from Michigan who really loves learning and is curious about life.

Madonna, on who she is, interview with *O, The Oprah Magazine*, January 2004.

I always thought of myself as a star, though I never in my wildest dreams expected to become this big. I knew I was born to it. I don't know why. I think people are named names for certain reasons, and I feel that I was given a special name for a reason. In a way, maybe I wanted to live up to my name.

Madonna, on living up to her name, interview with *New York Times*, June 1986.

I make my own work. I don't sit around waiting for other people to give it to me. I've had to do this to ensure myself constant employment. I honestly don't think I could just announce to Hollywood, 'OK, now I want to be an actress,' and then wait for people to give me movies. I also couldn't be just a recording artist who puts out a record once a year. I have to keep finding things for myself to do.

Madonna, on her workaholism, interview with *Rolling Stone*, June 1991.

I'm not an orphan, I wasn't sexually abused as a child, I don't let people take advantage of me, I don't drink myself into a stupor, and I'm not beholden to a man. I could cut my heart open and give people a million reasons to feel sorry for me, I haven't had an easy life. But I'm a survivor.

Madonna, on being a survivor, interview with *Los Angeles Times*, October 23, 1994.

First of all, I wanted to make a living. I was tired of being broke. But second of all, all I wanted was a song to get played on the radio. That's all I was praying for.

Madonna, on why she became a singer, interview with *New York Times*, June 2019

When I was younger, the first thing I wanted to be was a movie star. Then, I wanted to be a singer and then, I got into dancing more and really started concentrating on that. I just felt like I really needed a skill to go to New York with. I had to arm myself because I didn't know anyone in New York and I had never been here before. I loved to dance and I was really good at it so I figured, well, I can always start off as a dancer in New York and just take it from there.

Madonna, on her desire to dance, interview with *Rock Video*, February 1985.

Madonna has six children: Lourdes, Rocco, David, Mercy, Esther and Stella.

My first job, I was a drummer for the Breakfast Club. We made the circuit of all the shitty clubs. We played on the audition nights and the nights where you didn't get any money and you were the tenth band to play and you set up your shit at three in the morning and there were 10 people in the audience and people threw things at you. I went through all of that.

Madonna, on her first band, interview with *Rock Video*, February 1985.

One always thinks about England as being this repressed, tradition-based place, where everyone has this uptight prim way of relating to each other. But, in fact, Americans, who are known for being boisterous and straightforward, are puritanical, so it's a strange paradox.

Madonna, on her becoming "Her Madgesty of England", interview with *The Face*, August 2000.

**"**

When you're famous, people like to narrow you down to a few personality traits. I think I've just become this ambitious, say-whatever's-on-her-mind, intimidating person. And that's part of my personality, but it's certainly not anywhere near the whole thing.

**"**

Madonna, on having her reputation precede her, interview with *The Face*, August 2000.

I wanted to chase after boys on the playground, but the nuns told me I couldn't. Good Catholic girls don't chase after boys.

Madonna, on her Catholic education, interview with *Interview* magazine, May 1989.

66

# Sadness is a teacher, and happiness is really a gift.

99

Madonna, on life lessons, interview with
*Interview* magazine, May 1989.

In some respects I will never die. Because art is immortal. What we leave behind and what we create – the energy that we put out into the world is eternal. The physical body is assembled just like a chair or a building or a flower, but the revolutions we start, the people we affect and inspire, that is eternal. So, in that respect, we do achieve immortality, and that makes me less fearful.

Madonna, on her art as immortality, interview with *Rolling Stone* magazine, March 2015.

The first apartment I ever had all by myself was on Fourth Street and Avenue B, and it was my pride and joy, because it was the worst possible neighbourhood I could ever live in.

Madonna, on life in New York before fame, interview with *Rolling Stone*, November 1984.

# CHAPTER
# FOUR

# RAY OF LIGHT

During her tenure at the top of the charts, the often-imitated-but-never-bettered Madonna has shape-shifted from one reinvention to countless others and swam the entire length of music's gene pool, from rock and pop, R&B and EDM, to country and indie. All while wearing either very little or something wildly erotic (see: 1984).

Yes, Madonna's music was akin to gorgeous rays of light that always brightened up her fans, no matter what she did. Or said…

"

Fame is a double-edged sword. I grew up saying I wanted to be somebody. I tried to be different, tried to dress different. Finally, you get what you've been searching for all those years, and then you spend the rest of your life trying to hide. It's really weird. Now, I walk around the streets with your eyes down. Just establishing eye contact is like asking for it.

"

Madonna, on the harsh realities of fame, interview with *Time Out*, January 1989.

66

When I'm hungry, I eat.
When I'm thirsty, I drink.
When I feel like saying
something, I say it.

99

Madonna, on her life philosophy, interview with
*Los Angeles Times*, October 23, 1994.

In 2012, Madonna headlined America's iconic, and prestigious, Super Bowl XLVI Halftime Show.

It immediately became the most-watched Super Bowl halftime show ever. More than 114 million viewers tuned in to view the performance, millions more than for the game itself.

I want to be good to my body. I don't want to stay in the sun too much and eat lots of crappy food. I want to exercise because I want to stay healthy and look good for as long as possible. But I don't sit here wondering if I'll still be making videos when I'm 50. I hope that I'll have three children and that they'll be the centre of my life – not being on MTV.

Madonna, on career longevity and her health, interview with *Los Angeles Times*, October 23, 1994.

**"**

The dancefloor was quite a magical place for me. The freedom that I always feel when I'm dancing, that feeling of inhabiting your body, letting yourself go, expressing yourself through music. I always thought of it as a magical place... even if you're not taking ecstasy.

**"**

Madonna, on the power of the dance, interview with *Q Magazine*, March 1998.

**"**

I played guitar and keyboard to write.
But I got sick of bands. I felt like I
was getting nowhere with it. So, I
went into a studio on 8th Avenue
and 37th Street with Steve Bray and
made a demo. Between him and I,
we played all the instruments. We
made the tape ourselves, playing
everything and writing everything.

**"**

Madonna, on her first demo which got her noticed,
interview with *Rock Video*, February 1985.

I worked my butt off before I got where I got. I literally starved and lived on the street and ate out of garbage cans before any of this happened.

Madonna, on her work ethic, interview with *Rock Video*, February 1985.

In 1990, Madonna caused global "controversy" when she simulated masturbation on a bed during a performance of 'Like a Virgin' on her Blond Ambition World Tour.

At the time, the Pope called it "one of the most satanic shows in the history of humanity".

I can't completely disdain the song and video for 'Material Girl', because they certainly were important to my career. But talk about the media hanging on to a phrase and mis-interpreting the damn thing as well. I didn't write that song, you know, and the video was all about how the girl rejected diamonds and money. But God forbid irony should be understood.

Madonna, on "Material Girl" being misunderstood, interview with *Cosmopolitan*, February 1996.

> **"** When I'm ninety, I'll still be the Material Girl. I guess it's not so bad. **"**

Madonna, on "Material Girl", interview with *Cosmopolitan*, February 1996.

My daughter is a fan of mine but she doesn't want to be too obvious about it because I'm her mum and it's not cool. So she loves Beyoncé.

Madonna, on her children as fans, interview with *Observer Music Monthly*, November 2005.

> **"**
> I want to make people feel like they're inside a disco ball.
> **"**

Madonna, on her album *Confessions from a Dancefloor*, interview with *Rolling Stone*, December 2005.

Madonna has written
more than
20 children's books.

Her first publication,
*The English Roses*,
published in 2003, is
a story of rivalry
and friendship among
schoolgirls.

**"**

If my mother didn't die and I grew up with a feeling of wholeness and completeness and family, I probably would have stayed in Michigan and become a schoolteacher.

**"**

Madonna, on the death of her mother, interview with *Rolling Stone* magazine, March 2015.

"

When Britney went to kiss me, she just went for it. I tried to go with it so it wouldn't be weird. I'm a showgirl. After 20 years in show business, I've learned to roll with the punches.

"

Madonna, on kissing Britney Spears onstage at the 2003 MTV VMAs, interview with *O, The Oprah Magazine*, January 2004.

'Papa Don't Preach' is a message song that everyone is going to take the wrong way. Immediately they're going to say I am advising every young girl to go out and get pregnant. When I first heard the song, I thought it was silly. But then I thought, wait a minute, this song is really about a girl who is making a decision in her life. She has a very close relationship with her father and wants to maintain that closeness. To me it's a celebration of life.

Madonna, on "Papa Don't Preach", interview with *New York Times*, June 1986.

Just because I've taken my clothes off in public doesn't mean that I've revealed every inch of my soul.

Madonna, on baring her soul, interview with *Los Angeles Times*, October 23, 1994.

---

**66**

# My judgement is never based on the world's reaction.

**99**

Madonna, on not caring what her fans or critics think, interview with *Q Magazine*, December 1994.

---

I know there are many people who think I have no acting career. Because I'm a huge 'celebrity', I have a lot of baggage dragging behind me, and it's hard for people to disassociate the media portrayal of me when they're watching the film. Very often people either can't believe it's me playing a character. So, it's hard for people to separate, and I have the extra challenge of finding the role that will rise above all of that.

Madonna, on her movie characters, interview with
*Q Magazine*, December 1994.

**"**

I do look at old photographs
of myself and think, 'Someone
should have arrested me,
someone should have
stopped me from doing
my hair that way'.

**"**

Madonna, on her earlier photoshoots and career,
interview with *Q Magazine*, March 1998.

People don't want to like me. And that's because you're not supposed to be flirty unless you're an airhead. People say I look the way I do because I want to please men. I'm doing it because I like it. If I don't like it, no one's going to. I do it because it turns me on.

Madonna, on her earliest look, interview with *Record Magazine*, March 1985.

I have the answer to the meaning of life. We're here to share, to give, to love. When you die your physical body no longer exists, but your soul, and what you gave and how you loved goes with you.

Madonna, on the meaning of life, interview with *Q Magazine*, April 2003.

When I walk down the street anywhere people say, 'Oh, there's Madonna.' But in New York the cops are like, 'Hey, you're back!' It feels like I've come home.

Madonna, on New York as home, interview with *Observer Music Monthly*, November 2005.

Don't be fooled, not much has changed – certainly not for women. We still live in a very sexist society that wants to limit people. Since I started, I've had people giving me a hard time because they didn't think you could be sexual or have sexuality or sensuality in your work and be intelligent at the same time. For me, the fight has never ended.

Madonna, on sexism and ageism, interview with *Cosmopolitan*, May 2015.

Jean-Michel Basquiat was my boyfriend for a while. I remember getting up in the middle of the night and he wouldn't be in bed lying next to me; he'd be standing, painting, at four in the morning, this close to the canvas, in a trance. I was blown away by that – he worked when he felt moved.

Madonna, on artist and boyfriend Jean-Michel Basquiat, interview with *Interview* magazine, January 2015.

"

I couldn't be a success without also being a sex symbol. I'm sexy. How can I avoid it? That's the essence of me. I would have to have a bag over my head and over my body; but then my voice would come across, and it's sexy.

"

Madonna, on being sexy, interview with *Spin*, May 1985.

> **"**
>
> # Crucifixes are sexy because there's a naked man on them.
>
> **"**

Madonna, on crucifixes, interview with *Spin*, May 1985.

"

When you go to Catholic school, you have to wear uniforms, and everything is decided for you. Since you have no choice but to wear your uniform, you go out of your way to do things that are different in order to stand out. All that rebellion carried over when I moved to New York to become a dancer.

"

Madonna, on her Catholic school education, interview with *New York Times*, June 1986.

CHAPTER
**FIVE**

# GIRL
# GONE WILD

Fearless, provocative, controversial, misunderstood, Madonna has been a busy little beaver (no pun intended) for four decades, firmly resting her tongue in several cultural cheeks with little sign of slowing down as she passes her own sixth decade.

Even at her wildest, and most daring, Madonna was never less than thrilling, as you're about to find out...

It's flattering to me that people take the time to analyze me and that I've so infiltrated their psyches that they have to intellectualize my very being. I'd rather be on their minds than off.

Madonna, on her work, image and life being scrutinized, interview with *Vanity Fair*, April 1990.

So far my therapist has disapproved of everything I've done since I've started seeing her. That's why I haven't gone lately.

Madonna, on her psychologist and therapy sessions, interview with *Rolling Stone*, June 1991.

66

I'm very conscious of what my daughter is exposed to. There are going to be things that she's going to ask for that she's not going to get. If she wants a pair of Nike trainers I'm not going to make a stink about it, but she's not having 10 pairs. She's going to have to accept that.

99

Madonna, on not having spoilt children, interview with *Q Magazine*, April 2003.

Madonna's *Evita*, a musical about the life of Eva Perón, the former First Lady of Argentina, still holds the record for most costume changes in a film – 85!

In the film, Madonna wears 39 hats, 45 pairs of shoes, and 56 pairs of earrings.

I do think someone is protecting me. I don't know if it's an angel. It could be the devil.

Madonna, on angels and devils, interview with *Interview* magazine, June 1990.

That's my job. I'm in the world
of creating illusions and giving
people the ability to dream and
to be inspired or moved.
I don't want people to see the
labour behind it. Also, I was
trained that, as a dancer, no matter
how much you're suffering, your
face is always relaxed.

Madonna, on never letting people see you suffer,
interview with *Interview* magazine, January 2015.

When I did my *Sex* book, it wasn't the average. When I performed 'Like a Virgin' on the MTV Awards and my ass was showing, it was considered a total scandal. It was never the average, and now it's the average.

Madonna, on being ahead of the curve, interview with *Rolling Stone* magazine, March 2015.

**"**

What I've learned from all the controversy is that you can't expect everyone to get your sense of humour. But I've also learned that people eventually do catch on to what they didn't get at first. It's a nice surprise in the end for them when they do.

**"**

Madonna, on her sense of humour, interview with *New York Times*, June 1986.

People are becoming more aware that I have a brain in my head and a head on my shoulders and I am in control of myself, and I have a sense of humour.

Madonna, on people's perceptions of her, interview with *Vanity Fair*, December 1986.

I feel I've been misunderstood. I tried to make a statement about feeling good about yourself and exploring your sexuality, but people took it to mean that everyone should go out and have sex with everyone, and that I was going to be the leader of that.

Madonna, on being misunderstood, interview with *Los Angeles Times*, October 23, 1994.

There's a whole generation of women who cannot bring themselves to say anything positive about me even though I've opened the door for them, paved the road for them to be more outspoken. In fact, they slag me off any time anybody asks what they think of me or compare them to me.

Madonna, on starting a feminist revolution, interview with *Los Angeles Times*, October 23, 1994.

I see my influences everywhere. And I'm amused by it.

Madonna, on being an inspiration, interview with *Q Magazine*, December 1994.

> **"**
> Quick, tell me when the fun part of being famous kicks in.
> **"**

Madonna, on fame, *Evita*, interview with *Cosmopolitan*, February 1996.

Any mistakes I've made are war wounds I wear proudly because they've shaped me more than anything else. I can only hope that if I'm patient and diligent enough, if I continue to grow as an artist and a human being, people will come to realize that I'm not some callous, power-hungry, sex-crazed control freak who sings occasionally. They'll see me for what I am.

Madonna, on the real Madonna, interview with *Cosmopolitan*, February 1996.

I've never wanted to repeat myself. I don't ever want to repeat myself or make the same record twice. Yuck!

Madonna, on repeating herself, interview with *Q Magazine*, April 2003.

66

I arrived at a different time. Before the time of Svengalis holding talent searches: finding a girl that looks right and can carry a tune, and then figuring a way to market her. I'm not saying those girls can't grow into something, but I really don't know where we're going with the world. Everything's so homogenised.

99

Madonna, on the state of the music industry, interview with *Q Magazine*, April 2003.

"

It's funny that I've supposedly made my career out of being controversial, so now even my child-rearing and my spiritual life are freaking people out. It just goes to show that the media is not comfortable with what's not familiar.

"

Madonna, on being unable to win with the media, interview with *Rolling Stone*, December 2005.

66

As corny as it sounds, if
I didn't have some kind of
spiritual belief system, if I
couldn't find a way to make
sense out of the chaos in
the world around me – not
my personal chaos, but the
chaos in the world – I would
be a very depressed person.

99

Madonna, on finding Kabbalah, interview with
*Rolling Stone*, December 2005.

My nature is to provoke. I can't help myself. But it's always with good intentions.

Madonna, on her desire to provoke, interview with *Rolling Stone* magazine, March 2015.

**"**

I don't think my ex-husband [Guy Ritchie] approved of me kissing Britney Spears onstage. Or maybe he didn't understand it. Was it provocative? I think it was. I mean, now it wouldn't be.

**"**

Madonna, on that now-legendary kiss onstage with Britney Spears at the 2003 MTV VMAs, interview with *Rolling Stone* magazine, March 2015.

66

I hope I've been given the label of teacher. That's how I see myself now. Inspiring people and sharing what I've learned – that's the most important thing. It's what I was put here to do. All my fame and fortune have led to this one understanding: That I'm here to help people.

99

Madonna, on being regarded as a teacher, interview with *O, The Oprah Magazine*, January 2004.

A lot of people say I'm fearless,
I'm courageous, I take risks.
My job is to conquer my fears.
The irony of being a performer
is that I have huge insecurities.
People are shocked to hear
that I think my legs are fat or
I don't like the way I look. We
all have insecurities. We'd be
lying if we said we didn't.

"

Madonna, on having insecurities, interview with *O,
The Oprah Magazine*, January 2004.

Part of the reason I'm successful is because I'm a good businesswoman, but I don't think it is necessary for people to know that. I'm in charge of everything. People say no to me all the time, but I guess the balance is tipped in the yes direction. If they do say no, you can be sure there will be a tantrum to follow.

Madonna, on being the boss of her own business, interview with *Vanity Fair*, April 1990.

66

I don't do things because
I may be afraid of what
people might think. What
you see is what you get. I'm
not hiding anything. That
may explain my longevity.

99

Madonna, on her longevity in the music industry,
interview with *Vanity Fair*, April 1990.

Almost all of my songs are romantic. I don't write shocking, explicit lyrics.

Madonna, on her romantic lyrics, interview with *Cosmopolitan*, February 1996.

Before singing, dancing, synthesizing and guitar playing took centre stage in her life, Madonna was the drummer, and founding member, of two NY bands, Breakfast Club and Emmy.

The latter's music caught the attention of Sire Records founder Seymour Stein, who offered (only) Madonna a recording deal.

"

I'm not a reluctant pop
star. I'm very grateful and
happy for everything that
I have and for things when
they go well. On the other
hand, I've had enough of
the other side to know that
if it doesn't, I will survive
that and life goes on.

"

Madonna, on surviving fame, interview with
*Observer Music Monthly*, November 2005.

Madonna is one of the wealthiest musicians ever to express herself on stage. Her fame has generated a fortune with an estimated net worth of $850 million.

In 2023, Forbes named Madonna the richest female musician of all time. Not bad for a girl from Michigan.

**"**

# The word 'no'.

**"**

Madonna, when asked "What motivates you?",
interview with *Q Magazine*, May 2008.

Growing up in Michigan, I didn't really know what a gay man was. My ballet teacher [Christopher Flynn] was the first man – the first human being – who made me feel good about myself and special. He was the first person who told me that I was beautiful or that I had something to offer the world.

Madonna, on her movie *Filth and Wisdom* (2008) and her ballet teacher, interview with *Interview* magazine, February 2010.

It's good to get into arguments with people and have them say, 'You're crazy!' It helps you understand what you believe in.

Madonna, on being told she's "crazy", interview with *Interview* magazine, February 2010.

I'd like to know what those things are like. I'd really like to pee standing up.

Madonna, on penises, interview with *Rolling Stone*, June 1991.

# CHAPTER
## SIX

# MADAME X

Madonna's journey from fierce, anything-but-a-material-girl from Bay City, Michigan to her current position as our lady of the divine, Madame X, is nothing short of a miracle her religious namesake would approve of.

Madonna had the balls to change the world forever. For the better. And she did. And all she really did was spread one glorious gospel:

To thine own self be true…

Whenever I write about sex, I always do it tongue-in-cheek. That's the one thing that people misunderstand grossly about me.

Madonna, on being tongue-in-cheek, interview with *Rolling Stone* magazine, March 2015.

You know where my rebellion comes from – my Catholic upbringing. I was exorcising the extremes my upbringing dwelt on. Putting them up on the wall and throwing darts at them.

Madonna, on her Catholic School upbringing, interview with *Vanity Fair*, December 1986.

You mean they don't realize I'm a songwriter as well as a slut? It's the image that gets in the way. What am I supposed to do? I'm not going to put a sticker on the outside of the album that says, 'Listen! I wrote these songs!' You know, they pay attention to what they want to pay attention to.

Madonna, on image versus artistry, interview with *Songtalk*, June 1989.

I'm punished for having a sex life. For enjoying it and for saying that I enjoy it. I really think it's that simple.

Madonna, on the media's outrage at her reported promiscuity, interview with *Los Angeles Times*, October 23, 1994.

I don't think I sing like a woman. I sing like a girl, and it's a quality I never want to lose.

Madonna, on her singing voice, interview with *New York Times*, June 1986.

To her fans, Madonna Louise Ciccone is the Queen of Pop and the Mother of Reinvention.

However, she is also known under the disguise of several not-so-secret nicknames: Daisy, Esther, Little Nonni, M, Emmy, Madge and Brenda.

Do you know the reasons behind each of them?

# There is a wink behind everything I do.

Madonna, on being tongue-in-cheek, interview with
*Vanity Fair*, April 1990.

66

I wanted to be a nun. I saw nuns as superstars.

99

Madonna, on nuns, interview with *Rolling Stone*, June 1991.

I used to think of myself as a victim and whenever bad things happened I'd think, 'Oh, people are doing these things to me!' But everything that happened to me, I attracted to me and I brought it on myself. I am the master of my own fate.

Madonna, on creating her own fate, interview with *Juice*, April 1998.

I know it sounds clichéd, but I've had 20 years of fame and fortune, and I feel that I have a right to an opinion on what it is and what it isn't. All everyone is obsessed about at the moment is being a celebrity. I'm saying that's bullshit… and who knows better than me?

Madonna, on the horrors of celebrity, interview with *Q Magazine*, April 2003.

The press don't want me to be happily married and have a family.

Madonna, on the press, interview with *Q Magazine*, April 2003.

As the years go by you evolve. You think, 'Oh my God, having a song on the radio and being number one is the most important thing in the world', and then you get the shit kicked out of you and you think, 'I can't deal with this', and you realize that having a number-one record and being loved and adored isn't the most important thing in the world.

Madonna, on realizing what's important, interview with *Observer Music Monthly*, November 2005.

"

At the end of the day when I'm standing at the golden gates, I'm sure God doesn't give a shit how many records I've sold or how many number-one hits I've had. All he gives a shit about is how I behaved, how I treated people.

"

Madonna, on God and music, interview with *Observer Music Monthly*, November 2005.

Since the beginning of my career I've been told I have no talent, I can't sing and I'm a one-hit wonder. That was 22 years ago.

Madonna, on her critics, interview with *Observer Music Monthly*, November 2005.

---

**"**
You can negotiate with
a terrorist.
**"**

Madonna, when asked "What's the difference between
a terrorist and a pop star?", interview with *Observer
Music Monthly*, November 2005.

---

All my life I've been going out of my way to get my father's approval. And he's never been impressed.

Madonna, on her strained relationship with her father, interview with *Rolling Stone*, December 2005.

66

Guys get to do everything. Take their shirts off in the summer. They get to pee standing up. They get to fuck a lot of girls and not worry about getting pregnant.

99

Madonna, on men, interview with *Interview* magazine, June 1990.

I think that everyone should get married at least once, so you can see what a silly, outdated institution it is.

Madonna, on marriage, interview with
*Interview* magazine, June 1993.

The first real money I ever got was $5,000 from Sire Records, and the first expensive thing I bought was a Roland synthesizer. The next big money I got was publishing money for writing songs. I would get $1,000 for every song I wrote. I wrote most of the songs on my first album, so I got what seemed like a lot of money at the time.

Madonna, on her first big pay cheques, interview with *Spin*, May 1985.

"

If I wasn't doing what I'm doing, I would be a nun. The reason I'm not a nun is because you can't take your own name. How could I change my name? I have the most holy name a woman can have. But if I had to change my name, I'd use my confirmation name, Veronica. I chose her because she wiped the face of Jesus, which I thought was really dramatic.

"

Madonna, on being a nun, interview with *Spin*, May 1985.

Madonna, Prince and Michael Jackson – the Holy Trinity of '80s pop stars – were all born in the same year:

# 1958.

I get so much bad press because people associate a girl who's successful with a bimbo or an airhead. Sexy boys never get bad press. Do you think they'd bug Prince if he pulled out his dick on stage? If I ever did something like that, I'm the slut of the year.

Madonna, on gender double standards, interview with *Spin*, May 1985.

66

When people are busy
making music and dancing,
they're kind of too busy
to hate and fight. Music is
one of the great unifiers.

99

Madonna, on the value of music, interview
with *Interview* magazine, April 2008.